CATS
AND
WILD CATS

Text/Consultants: Dr. John Seidensticker and Dr. Susan Lumpkin
Illustrator: Simone End

Published by
The National Geographic Society
Reg Murphy, President and Chief Executive Officer
Gilbert M. Grosvenor, Chairman of the Board
Nina D. Hoffman, Senior Vice President
William R. Gray, Vice President and Director, Book Division
Barbara Lalicki, Director of Children's Publishing
Barbara Brownell, Senior Editor
Mark A. Caraluzzi, Marketing Manager
Vincent P. Ryan, Manufacturing Manager

Library of Congress Catalog Number: 96-068857
ISBN: 0-7922-3445-6

Produced for the National Geographic Society by Weldon Owen Pty Ltd
43 Victoria Street, McMahons Point, NSW 2060, Australia
A member of the Weldon Owen Group of Companies
Sydney • San Francisco

Chairman: Kevin Weldon
President: John Owen
Publisher: Sheena Coupe
Managing Editor: Ariana Klepac
Text Editor: Robert Coupe
Art Director: Sue Burk
Designer: Mark Thacker
Photo Researcher: Anne Ferrier
Production Manager: Caroline Webber

Film production by Mandarin Offset
Printed in Mexico

MY FIRST POCKET GUIDE

CATS
AND
WILD CATS

DR. JOHN SEIDENSTICKER
and DR. SUSAN LUMPKIN

**NATIONAL
GEOGRAPHIC
SOCIETY**

INTRODUCTION

From a 3-pound rusty-spotted cat to a 700-pound tiger, all cats are meat-eating hunters with deadly, sharp teeth, strong jaws, and flexible bodies. Small cats prey on birds, rats, and mice. Big cats hunt deer and antelope. If you watch your pet cat hunt a bird, you will see just how a tiger hunts a deer. After watching and slowly following its prey, a cat rushes to pounce, then kills with a bite to the neck.

Most cats are similar in other ways, too. For example, except for mothers with their young, most cats live alone. Adult males and females meet only so that they can breed. The rest of the time, cats keep out of each other's way. Only lions, male cheetahs, and feral cats live in groups.

Domestic, or house, cats and a few big cats like lions and tigers are some of the world's best known animals. But few people know anything about most of the 36 kinds of cats that exist in the world. Some couldn't be included in this book because only a few people have ever even seen them.

Of all the cats, only domestic cats are thriving. Wild cats are in danger from hunters who kill them for their fur and other body parts. They also suffer when people take over their habitats. To save wild cats, people must care more about them. You can help by sharing with your family and friends what you learn about cats in this book.

HOW TO USE THIS BOOK

This book is organized by kind of cat from biggest—tiger—to smallest—domestic cats. Each spread in this book helps you identify one kind of wild cat you might see in your local zoo, or one breed of domestic cat you might find in your neighborhood. There is information about the cat's size, color, appearance, and behavior. For each wild cat, "Where To Find" has a map that is shaded to show where the cat lives. For each domestic cat, the shaded map shows "Where It Came From." Discover an unusual fact about the cat in the "Field Notes," and see it in its natural environment in the photograph. If you find a word you do not know, look it up in the Glossary on page 76.

TIGER

 Slowly and silently, a tiger stalks a deer or pig until it is 40 or 50 feet away. Then, with a few explosive bounds forward, it pounces on its prey. Like all other cats, it kills animals with a bite to the neck.

WHERE TO FIND:
Tigers live in Asia, in many different kinds of habitats. They need cover to hide in and plenty of water to drink.

WHAT TO LOOK FOR:

✳ **SIZE**
A large tiger can be as long as a small sports car, not including the tail, and can weigh almost 800 pounds.

✳ **COLOR**
It is reddish orange with dark stripes. It is white on the underside.

✳ **BEHAVIOR**
It leaves a special scent on trees, to warn other tigers to stay out of its territory.

✳ **MORE**
It needs to eat 40 to 70 animals a year.

The tiger is the largest member of the cat family. It weighs as much as ten fifth-graders!

LION

 Related female lions and their young live in a group called a pride. These females keep other females out of their territory. Male lions visit and live in a pride for only a short time.

Anywhere from 3 to 40 lions, including males, females, and cubs, can make up a pride.

WHERE TO FIND:
Lions live in Africa and Asia, in open woodlands, grassy plains, savannas, and semi-deserts.

WHAT TO LOOK FOR:

✳ **SIZE**
A lion is between five and eight feet long, and has a tail that is longer than your leg.

✳ **COLOR**
Lions vary from light brown to dark, orangish brown.

✳ **BEHAVIOR**
After killing prey, adult males eat first, then adult females eat. Cubs usually get only the scraps.

✳ **MORE**
A strong, fit male has a long, sleek mane.

LEOPARD

Leopards are medium-size cats that prey on many kinds of animals, from goats and deer to small rats and mice. Their spotted coats help them to blend into the background, so they can sneak up on their prey.

FIELD NOTES

Black leopards have spots, just like other leopards, but you need to look closely to see them.

WHERE TO FIND:
Leopards live in deserts, tropical forests, and even in villages and city suburbs in Africa and Asia.

WHAT TO LOOK FOR:

✳ SIZE
Leopards are between three and six feet long, with tails two to four feet long.

✳ COLOR
A leopard has gray, rusty brown, or black fur, covered with dark spots.

✳ BEHAVIOR
It drags large prey into trees so that lions or wild dogs do not steal its meal.

✳ MORE
Because it can do without water for a long time, it can live almost anywhere.

Leopards are excellent climbers. They often laze around in trees after they have eaten their prey.

JAGUAR

With big feet, thick, short legs, and strong, solid bodies, jaguars are the biggest of the American cats. They roam the forests, hunting bite-size morsels such as birds, as well as meatier creatures such as wild pigs and other mammals.

FIELD NOTES

Jaguars are strong swimmers. They sometimes capture prey in the water, then drag it to land to eat.

When jaguars meet, they usually fight. These males are ready for combat.

WHERE TO FIND:
Jaguars live along riverbanks and lakeshores in thick forests in Central and South America.

WHAT TO LOOK FOR:

✳ **SIZE**
Jaguars are four to six feet long, and have two-foot-long tails.

✳ **COLOR**
Their fur is gold to rusty red with black spots circled by rose-shaped patterns.

✳ **BEHAVIOR**
With its strong jaws, a jaguar can rip open a turtle shell to get the meat inside.

✳ **MORE**
Jaguars hunt on the ground, but climb trees to rest in.

SNOW LEOPARD

Human mountain climbers need special equipment to climb as high as snow leopards go. They can live at 18,000 feet—almost as high as Mount Denali, the tallest mountain in North America.

WHERE TO FIND:

Snow leopards live in cold, rocky pastures, high up in the mountains of central Asia.

ASIA

WHAT TO LOOK FOR:

✳ SIZE
A snow leopard grows three to four feet long. Its tail is almost that long, too.

✳ COLOR
It has pale gray fur with brown spots circled with rose-shaped patterns.

✳ BEHAVIOR
It rests on cliff tops. From there it can spot blue sheep and ibex—its main prey.

✳ MORE
Its large front paws and strong chest muscles help it to climb rocks.

A snow leopard's long, thick fur keeps it warm in the cold areas where it lives.

CLOUDED LEOPARD

Tigers and leopards sometimes prey on clouded leopards. When these larger cats are nearby, clouded leopards stay in the trees. In areas without tigers and leopards, clouded leopards hunt safely on the ground.

FIELD NOTES

Clouded leopards run along the undersides of branches, gripping the tops with their wide feet.

WHERE TO FIND:
The clouded leopard lives in tropical forests in Asia. It hunts both in trees and on the ground.

WHAT TO LOOK FOR:

✳ SIZE
A clouded leopard is about three feet long. Its tail is almost that long, too.

✳ COLOR
It has grayish or yellowish fur covered with large, cloud-shaped markings.

✳ BEHAVIOR
It hunts pigs and orangutans, as well as small squirrels and birds.

✳ MORE
Its markings help it to blend into its surroundings, to hide it from enemies.

The clouded leopard has short, powerful legs to help it climb trees.

CHEETAH

 Have you ever watched a train go by so fast that it looked like a blur? That's what it's like to see a cheetah sprint after a gazelle. In seconds a cheetah can go from a standstill to more than 60 miles per hour.

WHERE TO FIND:
Cheetahs live and hunt mainly in open grasslands and bushy areas in parts of Africa and the Middle East.

AFRICA

WHAT TO LOOK FOR:

✳ SIZE
Cheetahs grow about 4 feet long, with tails two feet long.

✳ COLOR
A cheetah's short, yellow fur is covered with round black spots.

✳ BEHAVIOR
Cheetahs eat small- to medium-size animals, such as hares and gazelles.

✳ MORE
After a chase, a cheetah needs half an hour to catch its breath before it can eat.

Cheetah cubs stay with their mothers until they are 12 to 20 months old.

PUMA

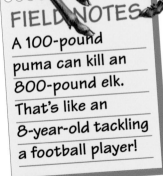

A puma is like a light breeze—you know it's there, but you can't see it. Even when it moves through open country, the puma always finds a clump of grass, a rock pile, or a shadow to hide in.

FIELD NOTES

A 100-pound puma can kill an 800-pound elk. That's like an 8-year-old tackling a football player!

The puma is also known as the cougar (KOO-ger), or mountain lion.

WHERE TO FIND:
Pumas live in North, Central, and South America, in forests, mountains, canyons, swamps, and grasslands.

WHAT TO LOOK FOR:

✳ SIZE
Pumas grow from 3 to 6 feet long, and have tails 20 to 30 inches long.

✳ COLOR
A puma's fur may be reddish brown, golden, or blue-gray.

✳ BEHAVIOR
Pumas mainly prey on deer, but also eat small animals such as ground squirrels.

✳ MORE
A puma's hind legs are longer than its forelegs. This makes it a good jumper.

JAGUARUNDI

Because it has a long body, short legs, a flat head, and small round ears like an otter, the jaguarundi is sometimes called an otter cat. It can climb, but stays mainly on the ground.

FIELD NOTES
Jaguarundi kittens born in the same litter may be different colors—either gray or reddish brown.

Jaguarundis are good swimmers and often take dips in rivers and streams.

WHERE TO FIND:
Jaguarundis live in the southern United States, Central America, and South America, in fields and forests.

NORTH AMERICA

SOUTH AMERICA

WHAT TO LOOK FOR:

✳ **SIZE**
A jaguarundi grows 20 to 30 inches long. Its tail is 10 to 20 inches long.

✳ **COLOR**
The jaguarundi's fur is either reddish brown or gray.

✳ **BEHAVIOR**
It eats small mammals. Unlike most cats, it sometimes eats fruit.

✳ **MORE**
Jaguarundis chirp and whistle. You may mistake these sounds for birdcalls.

LYNX

 The North American lynx feeds mainly on snowshoe hares, so wherever snowshoe hares live, so do lynxes. When they can't find their favorite food, they will eat mice, voles, and squirrels.

Lynxes climb trees to escape from predators such as pumas and wolves.

WHERE TO FIND:

North American lynxes live in evergreen forests that are snow-covered for most of the year.

WHAT TO LOOK FOR:

✳ SIZE
A lynx is about 3 feet long, and has a short tail. It weighs 18 to 22 pounds.

✳ COLOR
Its long, white-tipped fur is gray or light brown with small, pale spots.

✳ BEHAVIOR
Lynxes make their dens under logs or in similar sheltered places.

✳ MORE
Large, furry paws work like snowshoes to help lynxes walk on snow.

FIELD NOTES

If a lynx's ears are back and down, it is angry. If its ears are forward and high, it is calm.

Angry

Calm

25

BOBCAT

On a walk through the woods, you might pass a bobcat, but you probably won't see one. You might see its tracks in the snow. Quiet, shy bobcats are active mostly at night. They eat birds and mammals.

FIELD NOTES

Bobcats make their dens in bushes, hollow trees, and cracks in rocks. They often spend the daytime here.

As it stalks its prey, a bobcat stays close to fallen branches or other cover.

WHERE TO FIND:

NORTH
AMERICA

Bobcats live mostly in the United States, where they are found in wooded areas and city suburbs.

WHAT TO LOOK FOR:

✳ SIZE
A bobcat grows about two feet long and has a short tail.

✳ COLOR
Its fur is light gray to reddish brown with dark spots and stripes.

✳ BEHAVIOR
Bobcats hunt and kill white-tailed deer.

✳ MORE
Bobcat kittens find their way through dark woods by following their mother's white ear spots and white-tipped tail.

CARACAL

 Like ballet dancers, caracals (car-uh-CALLS) perform twisting leaps into the air. They are powerful, graceful runners that hunt mainly at night for birds, rodents, and large prey, such as antelopes.

WHERE TO FIND:

Caracals live in Africa and Asia. They are at home in dry areas on plains, rocky hills, and mountains.

WHAT TO LOOK FOR:

✳ SIZE
A caracal grows 2 to 3 feet long and has an 18- to 14-inch-long tail.

✳ COLOR
Its fur is golden brown to reddish, and creamy white on its belly.

✳ BEHAVIOR
The caracal is able to kill animals much larger than itself.

✳ MORE
A caracal's hind legs are longer than its forelegs, which helps it to jump high.

This caracal is
scratching a tree to
warn other caracals to
stay out of its territory.

SERVAL

 The serval has huge ears, which it uses to listen for the scurrying sounds of rodents in tall grass or underground burrows. When it pinpoints the sound, it leaps up and then pounces on its prey.

AFRICA

WHERE TO FIND:
Servals live in Africa, in woodlands and grasslands. They are always found close to water.

WHAT TO LOOK FOR:

✳ **SIZE**
A serval grows two to three feet long, not including its short tail.

✳ **COLOR**
Its golden coat has round, black dots and splotches. It is white underneath.

✳ **BEHAVIOR**
Servals sometimes make their dens in other animals' burrows.

✳ **MORE**
A serval often looks like it is bouncing on a pogo stick when chasing its prey.

Some people call servals "giraffe cats" because they are tall and have long necks, like giraffes.

FIELD NOTES

Servals scratch holes in mole rats' burrows. When a mole rat surfaces to repair the hole, the serval grabs it.

FISHING CAT

Strong and muscular, fishing cats are skillful swimmers. As their name suggests, they prey on fish and other water-dwelling creatures such as snakes and snails. They also eat birds or rodents that cross their path.

FIELD NOTES

Fishing cats sometimes dive headfirst into deep water to snatch fish up in their jaws.

Fishing cats poke among underwater rocks and plants to find snails and crayfish.

ASIA

WHERE TO FIND:
Fishing cats live in Asia, near marshes and along streams where there are plants and trees for cover.

WHAT TO LOOK FOR:

✳ **SIZE**
A fishing cat grows about three feet long, not including its short tail.

✳ **COLOR**
It has gray to grayish brown fur covered with small black spots.

✳ **BEHAVIOR**
Fishing cats catch fish in shallow water, with the claws on their front paws.

✳ **MORE**
The fishing cat's short, coarse fur stays fluffy even after a dip in the water.

LEOPARD CAT

Leopard cats sometimes live near farms, where they raid henhouses, and on plantations, where they are welcome because they catch mice and rats. They normally eat birds, small mammals, and fish.

The leopard cat gets its name because its fur has spots like a leopard's.

WHERE TO FIND:

The leopard cat lives in south and east Asia, wherever it can find tree cover and enough to eat.

WHAT TO LOOK FOR:

✳ SIZE
A leopard cat grows between 17 and 35 inches long. Its tail is half its body length.

✳ COLOR
Its fur is usually light brown with dark spots, bands, or blotches.

✳ BEHAVIOR
Leopard cats sometimes forage in caves, looking for fallen bats to eat.

✳ MORE
The leopard cat is a good swimmer. It is active mainly at night.

FIELD NOTES
Leopard cats hunt on tropical beaches for resting shorebirds and foraging rats.

RUSTY-SPOTTED CAT

Tiny and active, rusty-spotted cats can zip easily up trees and along branches. We know little about these smallest of all wild cats, but they probably hunt at night for birds, small mammals, reptiles, and insects.

WHERE TO FIND:
Rusty-spotted cats live in Asia. They are at home in moist forests, grasslands, and dry, scrubby areas.

ASIA

WHAT TO LOOK FOR:

✳ SIZE
This cat measures between 20 and 30 inches from head to tail. It is about 7 inches tall—the length of a pencil.

✳ COLOR
It has grayish fur tinged with orange. It has pale brownish spots and blotches.

✳ BEHAVIOR
Rusty-spotted cats sometimes kill chickens in farmyards.

✳ MORE
They spend most of their time in trees.

The rusty-spotted cat is thought to be most active at night, when it comes out to hunt for food.

FIELD NOTES

Rain brings rusty-spotted cats to the ground, where they hunt for frogs in puddles.

OCELOT

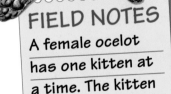 A tireless hunter, the ocelot spends more than 12 hours a day hunting for food. Sometimes it sits still, waiting for a rat or bird to pass under its nose. At other times, it creeps along slowly in search of prey.

FIELD NOTES

A female ocelot has one kitten at a time. The kitten stays with its mother for about two years.

This ocelot's staring eyes and alert posture show that it has spotted a meal.

WHERE TO FIND:

SOUTH AMERICA

Ocelots live in wooded areas in a small part of the United States and in Central and South America.

WHAT TO LOOK FOR:

✳ SIZE
Ocelots grow 26 to 39 inches long and have tails almost as long.

✳ COLOR
Their fur can be off-white or reddish gray, with dark spots and blotches.

✳ BEHAVIOR
Ocelots often hide in trees.

✳ MORE
An ocelot carefully plucks the feathers off a bird or peels the fur off a rat before eating it.

MARGAY

With their amazing agility, margays are the greatest acrobats of the cat family. A margay is a skillful climber; it runs up and down tree trunks and along branches to catch birds, rodents, and insects.

WHERE TO FIND:

CENTRAL AMERICA

SOUTH AMERICA

Margays live in tropical evergreen forests in Central and South America, where there is cover to hide in.

WHAT TO LOOK FOR:

✳ SIZE
Margays grow 18 to 31 inches long, not including their long tails.

✳ COLOR
Their gray to reddish fur is covered with brown or black streaks and spots.

✳ BEHAVIOR
Huge eyes and long whiskers help margays hunt in the dark.

✳ MORE
The margay's long tail helps the cat keep its balance in the treetops.

A margay's markings make it hard to see in the dappled forest light.

GEOFFROY'S CAT

Geoffroy's cats are good climbers and swimmers. Like most cats, their territories are large. Scientists found one male whose home area was about as large as 450 football fields put together!

FIELD NOTES
The Geoffroy's cat is the same color as its surroundings, so it can stay hidden while stalking its prey.

Geoffroy's cats hunt in trees and on the ground, for birds and rodents.

WHERE TO FIND:

SOUTH AMERICA

Geoffroy's cats live in South America in woodlands, open bush, rocky areas, and forests near water.

WHAT TO LOOK FOR:

✳ SIZE
Not counting their tails, Geoffroy's cats grow between 18 and 27 inches long.

✳ COLOR
Their fur is bright yellowish brown to silver-gray, covered in black spots.

✳ BEHAVIOR
They make dens in crevices in rocks, among tree roots, and in bushes.

✳ MORE
In some forest areas, Geoffroy's cats are all black.

PAMPAS CAT

With its big eyes and big pink nose, a pampas cat looks a bit like a clown. This long-legged cat is rarely kept in zoos, so scientists know little about how it lives. It is thought to be active mainly at night.

The pampas cat looks like a big, heavy house cat.

FIELD NOTES

On the Argentinian coast, pampas cats prey on penguin chicks in the nesting season.

SOUTH AMERICA

The pampas cat lives in South America in treeless grasslands, called pampas, and in moist forest areas.

WHAT TO LOOK FOR:

✳ SIZE
The pampas cat grows about two feet long, not counting its foot-long tail.

✳ COLOR
Its fur is yellowish white to brown or reddish to light gray, with yellow or brown spots or bands.

✳ BEHAVIOR
A pampas cat hunts on the ground for wild guinea pigs and large birds.

✳ MORE
It has a short mane around its neck.

PALLAS'S CAT

 Stocky with short legs, Pallas's cats are slow runners, but they can easily climb up steep cliff sides. They match the color of the rocks where they live, which makes it difficult for their enemies to see them.

WHERE TO FIND:
Pallas's cats live in Asia in cold, hilly deserts and rocky mountain areas where only light snow falls.

ASIA

WHAT TO LOOK FOR:

✳ SIZE
A Pallas's cat is about as long as your arm, not including its short tail.

✳ COLOR
Its gray to reddish fur is tipped with white. It has the longest fur of any cat.

✳ BEHAVIOR
It sneaks up on its prey, or ambushes it as it comes out of its burrow.

✳ MORE
In winter, the cat's fur grows extra long to keep it warm in the cold.

A Pallas's cat's long, fluffy fur makes it look much bigger than it really is.

FIELD NOTES
A flat head and low-set ears let a Pallas's cat stay hidden as it peeks over rocks to look for prey.

BLACK-FOOTED CAT

The black-footed cat hunts at night. It eats rodents, spiders, and insects. It runs away if disturbed, and so is rarely seen. It has black foot pads and fur on the bottoms of its feet.

FIELD NOTES
To hide and keep cool during the day, black-footed cats shelter in termite mound holes, or in empty fox burrows.

The black-footed cat crouches against rocks or bushes to escape its enemies.

WHERE TO FIND:

AFRICA

The black-footed cat lives in Africa in hot, dry areas where there are rocks, bushes, or grasses to hide in.

WHAT TO LOOK FOR:

✳ SIZE
The black-footed cat grows 14 to 18 inches long, not including its tail.

✳ COLOR
Its fur is tawny gold with black or brown spots and bars.

✳ BEHAVIOR
When alarmed, a mother black-footed cat calls to her kittens, which scatter.

✳ MORE
Although small, the black-footed cat is a fierce fighter.

SAND CAT

In the desert heat, sand cats often hunt at night and rest during the day. They use their excellent hearing to find prey, which includes rodents, birds, and snakes. They can go for years without drinking water. They get all the moisture they need from their prey.

FIELD NOTES

A sand cat stuns a snake with its paw, kills it with a neck bite, then swallows it.

A sand cat sits very still as it waits to pounce on its prey.

WHERE TO FIND:
Sand cats live in Asia and Africa in desert areas with scattered tufts of grass or small bushes for cover.

WHAT TO LOOK FOR:

✳ SIZE
A sand cat grows about 18.to 23 inches long, not including its long tail.

✳ COLOR
Its fur is sandy brown or gray, with darker rings on its tail and stripes on its legs.

✳ BEHAVIOR
Sand cats spend hot desert days in a cool burrow or in a hollow in the sand.

✳ MORE
They are hard to see against the sand, because they are the same color.

51

WILDCAT

Wildcats are the ancestors of domestic cats and look like big tabby cats. Wildcats eat mainly small rodents. People first tamed wildcats so that they would kill rats and mice around their homes.

African wildcat

It's easy to tell by looking at this European wildcat, that it is related to the domestic cat.

WHERE TO FIND:
Wildcats live in Europe, Africa, and Asia in forests, rocky mountains, grasslands, and dry, sandy plains.

WHAT TO LOOK FOR:

✳ SIZE
Wildcats are between 20 and 30 inches long with tails 8 to 14 inches long.

✳ COLOR
They vary from sand-colored to grayish brown, with brown or reddish stripes or dark spots.

✳ BEHAVIOR
Like domestic cats, wildcats make loud yowling sounds when they are courting.

✳ MORE
Wildcats usually live alone.

FERAL CAT

Feral cats are domestic cats that have adapted to living conditions without people. Because cats are good hunters, they sometimes survive. Female feral cats may live in groups, just like female lions do.

WHERE TO FIND:
You can find feral cats all over the world. Cities, farms, and wilderness areas are all places they live.

WHAT TO LOOK FOR:

✳ SIZE
Feral cats are about the same size as domestic cats.

✳ COLOR
They vary in color, but tabby, black, and orange are common.

✳ BEHAVIOR
As many as four females may have their kittens in the same place, then share the work of feeding and guarding them.

✳ MORE
Feral cats usually have short hair.

Feral cats often find a home in an abandoned building.

FIELD NOTES

In cities, garbage bins—and the rats and mice that they attract—provide food for feral cats.

ABYSSINIAN

The long, slender Abyssinian is an athletic cat that often runs and leaps around. It is sometimes called the "bunny cat" because the color of its short, silky fur is like a wild rabbit's.

The Abyssinian's fur looks all one color, but if you look closely you can see that each hair has stripes of two or three different colors.

AFRICA

WHERE IT CAME FROM:
In 1868 a soldier brought this cat to England from Abyssinia—which we now call Sudan and Ethiopia.

WHAT TO LOOK FOR:

✳ SIZE
Abyssinians are medium-size cats with long, slender legs, small feet, and long tails. The head is triangular.

✳ COLOR
They are usually reddish brown, but they can be other colors, such as gray.

✳ BEHAVIOR
The Abyssinian is a lively, active cat that likes to explore its surroundings.

✳ MORE
Its tail gets thinner toward the tip.

FIELD NOTES

When any cat is ready to attack, it holds its ears low and turned back, and wags its tail on the ground.

SIAMESE

Long, slim, and sleek, the Siamese cat is intelligent, and friendly to humans. Siamese kittens are born without the dark markings, called "points." These begin to show after a few months.

Siamese cats usually have blue eyes.

WHERE IT CAME FROM:
Siamese cats were brought to England and North America from Siam, now called Thailand, in 1871.

WHAT TO LOOK FOR:

✳ SIZE
The Siamese is a slender but muscular, medium-size cat with a triangular head.

✳ COLOR
Siamese are creamy white to pale brown with dark brown points on the ears, face, feet, and tail.

✳ BEHAVIOR
To get attention Siamese cats often make noisy yowling sounds.

✳ MORE
In hot climates, the points are paler.

BURMESE

Burmese cats are related to Siamese cats. Some Burmese have blue eyes, like their Siamese ancestors, but most have yellow or golden eyes. They are lively cats and often get into everything in the house.

Pupils in the dark

Pupils in the light

FIELD NOTES

The pupils of all cats' eyes are huge and round when it's dark, but shrink to narrow slits in sunlight.

ASIA

WHAT TO LOOK FOR:

✳ SIZE
Burmese are small cats with muscular, rounded bodies on long, slim legs.

✳ COLOR
The original color is glossy dark brown. Some cats have lighter colors.

✳ BEHAVIOR
Burmese cats are intelligent and curious. People say they can learn to open refrigerators to find snacks!

✳ MORE
A Burmese cat's tail has a rounded tip.

Most Burmese have short, dark brown, glossy fur like this cat.

BIRMAN

We do not know when the Birman breed was developed. You can see from its pale fur with dark points that it is related to the Siamese. Its long, silky fur may mean that is also related to the Persian.

FIELD NOTES

If any kitten wanders, its mother grasps the nape of its neck gently in her mouth and carries it back.

A Birman's eyes are blue like the eyes of its relative, the Siamese. It has pure white paws that look like gloves.

ASIA

WHAT TO LOOK FOR:

✳ SIZE
Birmans are large cats with thick legs, big paws, and bushy tails.

✳ COLOR
They have creamy golden to white fur with dark brown to gray markings.

✳ BEHAVIOR
Birmans are quiet, calm cats that are friendly to humans.

✳ MORE
The fur on a Birman's belly is fine and slightly wavy.

JAPANESE BOBTAIL

The short, curly tail that looks as if it has been "bobbed" (cut), gives the Japanese Bobtail its name. The tail is only about as long as a crayon, but a pom-pom of fur makes it look bigger.

ASIA

WHERE IT CAME FROM:

Japanese Bobtails were first brought to North America from Japan after World War II in 1945.

WHAT TO LOOK FOR:

✳ SIZE
Japanese Bobtails are medium-size cats. They are slim and long-legged.

✳ COLOR
They usually have white fur with patches of red, black, or both colors.

✳ BEHAVIOR
A Japanese Bobtail will often sit with one paw raised in the air as if making a sign to "come here."

✳ MORE
This cat is thought to bring good luck.

A Japanese Bobtail holds its short tail curled up close to its body.

PERSIAN

The Persian is more at home resting on a pillow than stalking a bird in the garden. A Persian has long, silky fur that needs a daily brushing by the cat's owner to keep it from getting tangled and dirty.

Some white Persians have one blue eye and one orange eye.

WHERE IT CAME FROM:
In the 1860s the first Persian cats were brought to Europe from Persia, part of Asia now called Iran.

WHAT TO LOOK FOR:

＊ SIZE
Persians have large, rounded bodies and short, thick legs. They have short, fluffy tails and flat faces.

＊ COLOR
Persians can be silver gray, white, or many other plain or mixed colors.

＊ BEHAVIOR
Persians are quiet, calm, and rarely active. They seldom show their claws.

＊ MORE
They have small ears and large eyes.

FIELD NOTES

All cats' tongues are covered with tiny hooks that brush the fur as they lick it to groom.

BRITISH SHORTHAIR

 The British Shorthair is a strong, intelligent cat that gets along with people. It is a sturdy-looking cat with a short, thick tail. The British Shorthair gets its name from its short, thick, velvety fur.

WHERE IT CAME FROM:

GREAT BRITAIN

In 1871, the first British Shorthair was bred from street cats chosen for their good looks and behavior.

WHAT TO LOOK FOR:

✳ SIZE
The British Shorthair is a short-legged cat with a broad chest and a short, thick neck. The head is big and round.

✳ COLOR
Colors include tabby, white, black, and calico.

✳ BEHAVIOR
These cats are good hunters that make sure no mice live in your house.

✳ MORE
Their eyes are usually orange.

Tabby—dark spots on a light background—is the natural pattern of a cat's coat. It is the most common color for domestic cats.

FIELD NOTES
Cats of many breeds can be calico—with patches of white, black, and orange fur. Only female cats have calico coloring.

MANX

Most Manx cats have no tail. Some have short tails and are called "Stubbies." Others have tails almost as long as normal cats and are called "Longies." Cats use their tails for balance, but the Manx does just fine without one.

Resting

Walking

Sniffing or biting

FIELD NOTES

All cats hold their whiskers in different positions, depending on what they are doing at the time.

WHERE IT CAME FROM:
The Manx cat comes
from the Isle of Man,
which is off the coast of
Great Britain.

WHAT TO LOOK FOR:

✳ **SIZE**
The Manx is a stocky cat with short legs.
Its rump is higher than its shoulders. Its
head is big, round, and wide.

✳ **COLOR**
A Manx can be almost any color.

✳ **BEHAVIOR**
Manx cats run like rabbits because their
hind legs are longer than their forelegs.

✳ **MORE**
The Manx has a thick coat of fur that
stands out from its body.

A Manx that
has no tail at
all is called a
"Rumpy."

71

RUSSIAN BLUE

You can see from the Russian Blue's long, slender body and triangular head that it is related to the Siamese and other cats from Asia. It has thick, soft, short fur that stands out from its body like a seal's fur.

FIELD NOTES

All cats are very agile and have a good sense of balance. They could almost walk along a tightrope.

EUROPE

WHERE IT CAME FROM:
The Russian Blue was brought to England on ships from the port city Archangel, in Russia.

WHAT TO LOOK FOR:

✳ **SIZE**
A Russian Blue's thick fur makes it look bigger than it is. It has long legs with small paws. Its tail is long and thin.

✳ **COLOR**
Its silky, plush coat is gray to blue gray.

✳ **BEHAVIOR**
It is a quiet, calm, and gentle cat that gets along well with people. You can hardly hear its call.

✳ **MORE**
Russian Blues have green eyes.

A Russian Blue perks up its ears to listen to sounds.

AMERICAN SHORTHAIR

With long, sturdy legs and heavy feet, American Shorthairs travel easily over any kind of ground. They have big, round heads with full cheeks and small ears.

The eyes of a solid black Shorthair are golden. Shorthairs of other colors can have blue or green eyes.

NORTH AMERICA

Shorthaired cats came to North America from Europe. American Shorthairs were first bred in the United States.

WHAT TO LOOK FOR:

✳ SIZE
American Shorthairs are strong cats with big chests and shoulders.

✳ COLOR
They can be orange, white, or gray, or any of more than 20 colors.

✳ BEHAVIOR
American Shorthairs get along well with people. They are good hunters.

✳ MORE
They have large, heavy paws and medium-length tails.

GLOSSARY

Ambush To attack by surprise from a hiding place.

Breed A special type of domestic animal developed by people. A Siamese is a "breed" of domestic cat.

Climate The usual weather in a place.

Communicate To send messages.

Courting When an animal is trying to attract and win a mate.

Cover Anything that hides or protects an animal, such as trees or rocks.

Environment An animal's surroundings.

Forage To search for food.

Habitat The place where an animal lives that provides food, water, shelter, and other things an animal needs to survive.

Ibex A wild goat.

Mate When an adult male and female come together to produce young.

Mole rats Small, ratlike animals that live underground.

Orangutan A large, tree-living ape with long red fur and long arms.

Peccary A piglike animal.

Pika A small, rabbitlike animal.

Plantation A large farm on which a few kinds of crops are grown.

Predator Any animal that hunts other animals for food.

Prey Any animal that is hunted by other animals for food.

Savanna A huge area of grassland with few trees, found in parts of tropical Africa.

Scrub A dry area with small bushes and low trees.

Stalk To follow slowly and quietly in order to catch and kill.

Tapir A large mammal with short legs and a long nose like a short trunk.

Territory The place where an animal or group of animals lives. Animals defend their territory from other animals of the same type.

Thicket A place where bushes and small trees grow very closely together.

Viper A poisonous snake.

INDEX OF
CATS AND
WILD CATS

ABOUT THE CONSULTANTS

Dr. John Seidensticker is Curator of Mammals at the National Zoological Park, Smithsonian Institution. A wildlife ecologist, he has studied tigers, pumas, leopards, and other large mammals. Long active in wildlife conservation, he is a member of the National Fish and Wildlife Foundation's Save the Tiger Fund Council.

Dr. Susan Lumpkin is Director of Communications at Friends of the National Zoo, Washington, D.C., and editor of *ZooGoer* magazine. She is also a freelance writer specializing in wildlife subjects. Studying animal behavior, she received her Ph.D in biological psychology.

PHOTOGRAPHIC CREDITS

front cover The Photo Library, Sydney/David Hiser **back cover** Bruce Coleman Ltd./Hans Reinhard **half title page** Images of Africa Photobank/David Keith Jones **title page** Marc Henrie **4** NHPA/Yves Lanceau **5** DRK Photo/Tom & Pat Leeson **7** Tom Stack & Assoc./E.P.I. Nancy Adams **8–9** Ardea London/C. Clem Haagner **10–11** Planet Earth Pictures/Roger de la Harpe **12–13** Bruce Coleman Ltd./Luiz Claudio Marigo **15** Ron Austing **17** NHPA/Andy Rouse **19** Planet Earth Pictures/Anup & Manoj Shah **21** DRK Photo/Tom & Pat Leeson **23** Planet Earth Pictures/Carol Farneti **24** The Image Bank/Joseph van Os **27** Oxford Scientific Films/Alan & Sandy Carey **29** Bruce Coleman Ltd./Rod Williams **31** Planet Earth Pictures/Jonathan Scott **33** FLPA/Terry Whittaker **34** Animals Animals/Michael Dick **36** FLPA/Terry Whittaker **39** Planet Earth Pictures/Carol Farneti **41** Ardea London/Francois Gohier **43** FLPA/F.W. Lane **44** Animals Animals/Michael Dick **47** Animals Animals/Michael Dick **49** Bruce Coleman Ltd./Gerald Cubitt **51** FLPA/E. & D. Hosking **53** Bruce Coleman Ltd./Gunter Ziesler **55** Auscape/Jean Paul Ferrero **56** Ardea London/Jean Paul Ferrero **58–59** Auscape/ Jean Michel Labat **60–61** Bruce Coleman Ltd./Hans Reinhard **63** Auscape/Jean Michel Labat **65** NHPA/Yves Lanceau **66** Bruce Coleman Ltd./Hans Reinhard **68** Bruce Coleman Ltd./Hans Reinhard **71** Animals Animals/Robert & Eunice Pearcy **73** Animals Unlimited **75** Animals Animals/Renee Stockdale **76** Tom Stack & Assoc./John Shaw **77** FLPA/Terry Whittaker **78 (top)** Bruce Coleman Ltd./Jane Burton **78 (bottom)** Planet Earth Pictures/Jonathan Scott **79** Bruce Coleman Ltd./Hans Reinhard.